FINDING OUT

CONTENTS

The night sky with its countless number of stars.

How many stars are there?

The number of stars in the sky has often puzzled people in the past, but so far, no answer to the question has yet been found. The universe is incredibly large. Five to six thousand stars can be seen from Earth with the naked eye and 100,000 with the aid of a telescope.

Observatories have special glasses, called telescopes, through which over 50 million stars can be seen and observed. The broad band of light spread out across the sky at night is called the Milky Way or the galaxy.

Our Earth and our solar system are only a small part of it and the Milky Way itself is one of many galaxies scattered throughout the universe. Astronomers think that there are over 100 billion suns in existence, each one having its own system around it. The stars are so far away from each other that it is impossible to guess their number.

Many more can be seen with a telescope than with the naked eye.

Why can't we fly to the stars?

The stars are so far away from each other that too many noughts would be needed to express distances in kilometres. Instead, distances in space are measured in light years. One light year represents the number of kilometres travelled by light in one year. Light moves at a tremendous pace, covering 300,000 kilometres per second, that is, around 100 billion kilometres in one year.

With the exception of the sun, the nearest star to our Earth is more than 40 billion kilometres away. The twinkling light seen from Earth has had to travel for at least four years before being seen. A star has even been discovered, the light of which takes more than 2 billion years to reach Earth. A human being lives for about 70 years which is not long enough for a journey to the stars. Such a flight would last for several human lifetimes.

The sun has set: the clouds are still slightly lit up.

Where does the sun go during the night?

You have probably played with a ball on the end of a piece of string sometime; if so, you must have felt the ball pulling on the string. The same thing happens with the Earth — it turns around the sun but in this case there is no string to hold it. Yet the Earth does not exert any pull on the sun; quite the opposite — the sun attracts the Earth. This is known as the gravitational force of the sun and is the reason why the Earth always follows the same orbit around the sun. The Earth also turns around itself. Our country turns with the Earth at a rate of about 1000 kilometres per hour. This is why the Earth does not always face the sun in the same way. When the side facing the sun is lit up it is day. Thus, the opposite side is not lit up and so it is night. At this point, the sun is on the other side of the Earth; as this rotates, it is day once again.

Why can't we stare at the sun?

In the past, many people worshipped the sun. They thought that the sun was a god. Without the sun, the Earth would die. The sun is a large luminous star. It looks like a great ball of fire but is, in fact, a ball of gas. These gases are so hot that they emit a white light. The sun's light, which we see as white, is actually made up of a mixture of colours: red, orange, yellow, green, blue, indigo and violet. (This is what you see when looking at a rainbow.) When the light emitted by the different colours reaches us, it appears to be white.

When you read, this white page does not blind you. But if the sun struck the paper, you would be completely blinded. Your eyes would hurt. That is why you should never look directly at the sun when it is high in the sky. You could do serious damage to your eyes; you even risk becoming blind.

The sun's light is blinding.

Why can't we live on the moon?

The lunar surface was seen through powerful telescopes a long time before the first man walked on it. The lunar surface is easy to see because the moon has no atmosphere.

The atmosphere surrounding the Earth is made up mostly of gases, the most important two being nitrogen and oxygen. Oxygen is vital for all living things, plants as well as animals and human beings. Without it, no life would be possible.

The moon has no oxygen, so it is impossible to live there. Another reason is that the lunar surface is covered with craters, mountains, ravines and seas. Telescopes and lunar maps give us all this information. But the lunar seas are empty. They contain no water. The latin word *mare* ("sea") describes the shape of the lunar landscape only. Hence, there is no life at all on the moon.

The moon buggy travels over the moon's surface.

Why can't an aeroplane fly to the moon?

No travel guide advertises flights to the moon. Why should this be? Men have already been to the moon. Yet they did not go by aeroplane. They travelled in a space capsule launched by a rocket. An aeroplane needs air to fly, the air found in our atmosphere. This air prevents the aeroplane from falling. The pressure exerted by the air keeps the machine in the sky. There is no atmosphere around the moon, so there is no air either. A normal aeroplane could not fly in these conditions. A very special aeroplane fitted with rockets is required in order to escape the gravitational forces of the Earth. This special vehicle must also be provided with heat shields to protect it from the radiation emitted in space and the friction forces in the atmosphere. Two countries have the most advanced rocket technology: the United States of America and the Soviet Union.

The space capsule flies into space.

Why isn't the moon always round?

It takes approximately 27 days for the moon to turn around the Earth. It also pivots around its own axis and always presents the same side to Earth. The moon may be perfectly round or it may be crescent shaped or appear as a half moon. In actual fact, it does not change shape at all, the different shapes being known as lunar phases. The moon gives out no light of its own but reflects the light of the sun which illuminates it. During its orbit around the Earth, the moon regularly passes between Earth and sun. At this point, the face lit up by the sun has its back to the Earth. The moon is completely black. This is known as the new moon. One week later, the right half is lit up; this is called the moon's first quarter. After another week it is fully lit and known as the full moon. During the third week, the volume becomes reduced again, only the last quarter or the left half being visible this time.

A crescent moon above the trees.

When the sun shines, the sea and the sky are often blue.

Why isn't the sky always blue?

We would like the sky to be always blue and the sun to shine so that the weather was fine all the time. Yet this is not the case. When the sun rises or sets, the sky appears to be all sorts of colours, ranging from pink to violet and sometimes even pale green.

The sun is also frequently hidden by cloud. When the sky is cloudy, the air is very humid. The clouds are often different colours and different shapes. They are made up of an incalculable number of water droplets and ice crystals.

Some people understand cloud patterns and can tell whether or not the weather will remain fine. Sometimes, the clouds are white and move about very slowly, high in the sky. These clouds generally mean good weather. Strips of black cloud low in the sky often bring rain and gusts of wind.

The Earth is covered with mountains and valleys.

Why aren't there mountains everywhere?

A long time ago, roughly the same thing happened on Earth as when you build a sandcastle on the beach. You make tracks and channels around which small piles of sand accumulate. But what happened on Earth took much longer and was on a much larger scale.

The Earth's crust changed over millions of years. Rivers pushed and eroded the land; various layers of the Earth's crust collided, thus forming mountains and valleys. The burning core of the Earth pushed volcanoes to the surface. Lava outflow solidified and layers became superimposed.

In other places, during the course of several thousand years, wind eroded the mountains and carried the particles elsewhere. Powerful forces from both inside and outside the Earth then pushed, folded and froze the Earth's crust.

High peaks are covered with snow.

Are there any mountains higher than the sky?

No, there are not. That's really impossible. The atmosphere around our Earth is about 30 kilometres thick. Extra-terrestrial space begins beyond that point.

Mont-Blanc in France is Europe's highest mountain: it is 4810 metres high, while the highest mountain in the world is Everest, in Asia, at 8880 metres.

Why do some peaks seem to reach the sky? You must have seen photographs of mountains in which the peak could not be seen. This is not impossible. Sometimes, the clouds are not very high in the sky. They move so far down that they cover the mountain tops. This is known as low cloud. At times, the clouds are so low that they seem to be resting on the ground. You are unable to see the things around you very clearly.

These clouds are called cumulus.

Where do clouds come from?

All clouds, with the exception of those emitted from factory chimneys containing dirt and soot, are made up chiefly of water. The sun heats up the oceans, lakes and rivers until the top layers are changed into steam. This steam rises. In the upper layers of the atmosphere it is very cold and the steam changes back into water droplets. These remain fixed together and float around in the form of clouds. Should a cloud then rise still further to where it is even colder, the drops of water freeze to form ice crystals.

When the cloud becomes too heavy, it returns to the lower layers, melts and falls as rain. The water once again reaches the oceans, lakes and rivers as well as the Earth, makes plants and trees shoot up and provides liquid for people and animals to drink. This evaporation and falling process is called the water cycle.

Why does it become windy?

The Earth is surrounded by a jacket of air called atmosphere. You don't see air, but you can feel it when it moves. This is known as wind. The air moves as a result of the Earth turning. The wind caused by the Earth's rotation always blows in the same direction in certain specific areas. This is known as constant wind.

There are other types of wind, for instance between two areas in which there is a great difference in temperature. Air rises when it is very hot. The vacuum left by this air is filled by air elsewhere. Cold air is heavier than hot air. Whilst hot air rises, cold air falls.

Changing winds are those which do not always blow in the same direction and in the same region; they do not appear on a regular basis. Tempests are very violent winds which may cause a great deal of damage.

Wind moves above water and land.

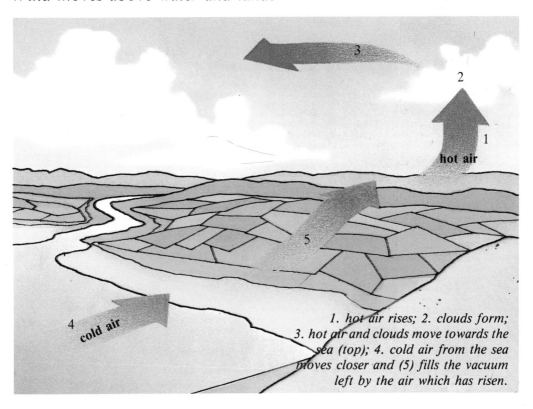

1. hot air rises; 2. clouds form; 3. hot air and clouds move towards the sea (top); 4. cold air from the sea moves closer and (5) fills the vacuum left by the air which has risen.

Why does it snow only in winter?

In the areas in which we live, it snows only in winter as this is the season in which we have the coldest weather. We have already explained how clouds are made up of water vapour from oceans, lakes and rivers. In the upper atmosphere, where it is much colder, the vapour turns to ice which sticks together. That is why it often snows all year round on high mountain peaks; in the Himalayas, Northern Spain or Switzerland, for example, where it is always cold enough.

In summer, it rains because the clouds become heavy. The ice crystals have to travel a long way before reaching the lower warmer levels where they then melt.

In winter, the air is colder, the vapour freezes more quickly and the clouds remain lower. Ice crystals no longer melt during their descent and fall as snowflakes.

Winter scene: what fun it is to go sledging!

Why is lightning dangerous?

Lightning is an enormous spark. It happens as a result of a build-up of electricity in the clouds. When a cloud is charged with too much electricity and a neighbouring cloud has less, lightning flashes until the electric charge in the two clouds is equal.

Sometimes, the electricity will simply disappear because there are no other clouds in the area. At this point, the thunderbolt shoots down to Earth and becomes a danger. It can strike anything, but always veers towards high points such as trees and church spires. In the absence of these high points, it strikes the ground. As the thunderbolt moves, it carves a sort of tunnel through the air. This tunnel fills with cold air, making a violent rumbling sound as it does so. This thunderclap is not at all dangerous. Thunderbolts, lightning and thunder are the three elements making up a storm.

Lightning zig-zags in the sky.

Why does water change to ice?

There is always the same amount of water on earth. It takes different forms, being in a liquid, gas or solid state. Water is the liquid state; water vapour is the gas state (think of a kettle in which water boils); and ice is the solid state.

When does water change to ice? The temperature has to fall below 0°C (0 degrees Celsius). At this point, we say it freezes. When the water temperature drops below 0°C (0 degrees Celsius), water freezes; this means that water changes from a liquid to a solid state. If you leave a bucket or bowl in the garden, you will see a thin layer of ice formed over the surface. Should it continue to freeze or the temperature drop suddenly to several degrees below zero, the bucket or bowl will contain a block of ice. Stagnant water freezes more quickly than running water as it remains still. On freezing, water takes up more space.

If it is safe enough, people skate on solid ice.

A desert is a vast expanse of dry, arrid country.

What is a desert?

A desert is a region totally or partly devoid of greenery. It is generally too dry for anything to grow. The soil is made up either of dry sand, stones and rocks, or it contains salt at certain points. In this case, nothing grows; no life is possible.

Most of the large deserts are the result of dry conditions. The main deserts are around the tropics, in both the northern and southern hemisphere (latitude 23.5 degrees north and 23.5 degrees south).

The air in the tropics is heated by the high temperature found there; it rises up into the sky, then falls, bringing with it very little rain. The Sahara in Northern Africa, the Gobi desert in China, the Kalahari desert in South West Africa and the Australian desert are some of those formed as a result of dry conditions. The Sahara is the largest desert in the world.

When it rains too much, it can sometimes cause flooding.

Why does it rain?

We have already explained the origin of snow and clouds. Water from the earth evaporates and rises up into the sky. The cold air of the upper atmosphere converts the vapour into droplets of water. These float close to each other, forming clouds. When a cloud becomes too heavy, it falls to Earth in the form of rain. The clouds may rise further and freeze when in contact with even colder air. Under the effect of the cold, the particles making up the cloud stick to each other to form flakes. In winter, when the temperature falls below 0°C (0 degrees Celsius), the clouds fall in the form of snowflakes. They do not melt. However, when the weather becomes warmer, it rains. The rain ensures a relatively constant level of humidity on Earth. If the rain were to cease, everything would dry up. So, the process of water escaping in vapour form and returning to Earth as rain is an essential one.

An impenetrable virgin forest.

What is a virgin forest?

A virgin forest is a very large and very dense wood. It is very difficult to get through as there are no paths. The trees, bushes, creepers and other plants are entangled together. Tree trunks and branches are all intertwined. Rivers often provide the only practical means of getting through. The forests are very dark, as the sun cannot penetrate the foliage. However, vegetation is luxurious due to abundant rainfall. It is very humid and unhealthy for human beings. Virgin forests still exist in the tropics — along the Amazon in South America, for instance. At the present time, forests are gradually being cut down. The home of great numbers of monkeys, parrots and snakes is becoming increasingly restricted in area. The virgin forests of Africa and Asia are also inhabited by elephants. The old European forests have been cleared and converted to cultivated land over the years.

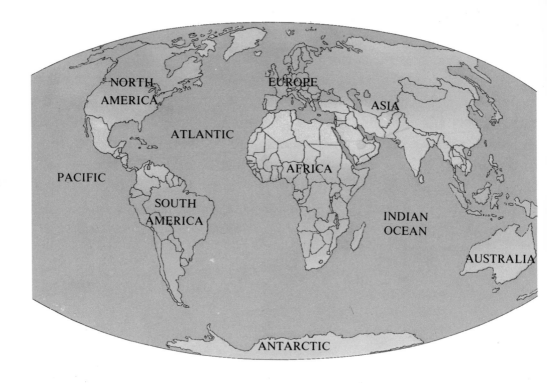

The world is divided into countries.

Why are there so many countries in the world?

When you look at a world map, you see mountains, seas, lakes and rivers. Nowadays these natural barriers no longer prevent us travelling. We have aeroplanes and high-powered boats, we can build tunnels through and roads across mountains. It was not like that a few thousand years ago. The mountain chains, lakes, wide rivers and oceans were impassable and provided natural frontiers for the regions which they enclosed. The inhabitants of each area had their own customs and their own way of life. The natural conditions under which they lived e.g. climate, type of soil, absence or presence of water, forests, etc. determined the types of occupation which they had.

Over the years, several groups came together and appointed a leader or a king. They also established artificial frontiers. To pass from one country to another, you cross the border between the two.

Why are people not all the same?

Countries and regions are all different from each other. There is a good deal of difference between hot regions, the tropics and the poles in particular. These three points on the globe are separated by a multitude of countries and regions in which climate, temperatures and conditions vary considerably. People who are born and grow up in these areas belong to them. They have learned how to make the most of their country. Their bodies have adapted to the environmental conditions. Dark-skinned people tolerate sun very well. Northern people are used to the cold and have always worn leather and wool clothing to protect themselves. Eating habits also vary.

As people now travel and move around a good deal, they change their customs as well as their clothing and eating habits, their beliefs and their way of life.

Climate determines the inhabitants' way of life.

What happens to the food which we eat?

The food which we eat undergoes great changes inside our bodies. These changes allow the blood to take the elements it needs and relay them to the different organs. It is thanks to this process that our bodies function the way they do. We start off by chewing food with our teeth. Here, food is mixed with saliva which helps it to slip down the throat more easily. This is the first stage. As it proceeds through the digestive system — stomach, intestines, gall-bladder and pancreas — it is split up into substances which are readily assimilated by the blood. Each organ has its own small "laboratory" which prepares a special substance for the blood. When the digestive process is finished, some unwanted products remain in the body. This waste is eliminated through the intestines and the bladder in the from of excrement and urine.

The food we eat is converted by the digestive organs.

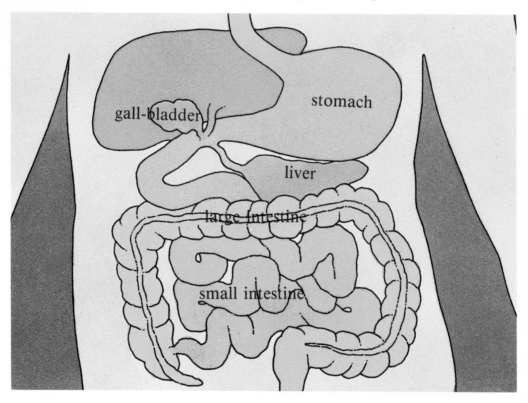

How do we grow into adults?

The adult stage means something different in the case of humans than it does for animals. In a human being, feelings and thoughts develop in addition to body growth. These two elements are partly or completely missing in animals. On the other hand, each type of animal masters at least one human activity better than Man does: a dog has a better scent, a monkey can climb better, a cat has a very fine sense of hearing, etc. But Man has all these aspects and "reason" besides. The learning process requires a great effort on the part of the child. A calf can walk right from the moment of birth, puppies run about after a few days. A child has more difficulty in learning because his mind and his feelings are developing at the same time. Animals do not speak, a child must learn a language. Human growth is both physical and psychic, hence progress is very gradual.

Children develop and become adults.

Why do we need sleep?

In nature, everything conforms to very strict rules. The sun follows rain, night follows day. Plants and animals obey these laws too. They go to sleep at a certain time and wake up at a certain time. The same thing applies for human beings, but Man is unique in that he does not respect Mother Nature's laws in the same way as other living creatures do. Yet Man must also rest. When he sleeps, his body rests, the blood rate slows down and he breathes more deeply. He feels tired. When he wakes up, he is fresh and alert once again, he can think more clearly. During the period of sleep he may or may not dream a good deal, but he will forget all that has gone on either inside his own body or in the environment around him. People who don't have enough sleep may become ill. Sleep is as essential as food. Whilst a child is growing it needs a lot of rest.

All living creatures need sleep.

Language is made up of sounds and gestures.

Why don't we all speak the same language?

Language is closely related to where we have been born and brought up. We have already explained that the large number of countries are the result of natural borders which define the territories of the various peoples. These people all have their own customs and their own language, i.e. their own sounds. The nature of these sounds depends on the environment: in places subject to a good deal of wind, people had to speak very loudly to make themselves heard. Many words are based on natural sounds such as whistling, thundering, chirping, twittering. Each language depends to a large extent on the living conditions during the time in which it first began. When contact between different peoples first started, words were borrowed from neighbours. That is why some words are similar in many languages. Some languages are spoken throughout the world.

Writing is essential to the growth of civilisation.

Why can't some people read and write?

We have a law in our country which requires all children of a certain age to attend school. This law also specifies what should be learned. But the same does not apply in all countries.

In the developing countries, known as the Third World, not everyone can read and write. People are unable to learn as not enough of their number know how to read and write and hence to teach others. That is why member countries of the United Nations — an organisation based on mutual assistance — all make their contribution towards improving the situation.

Many eastern countries require fewer people who can read and write than western ones, as science and industry are not so far advanced. There is always some learned person or priest who can read or write a letter. Fortunately, things are beginning to change.

Famine still claims too many victims.

Why do so many people still suffer from hunger?

The hunger situation in the world closely follows the reading and writing pattern. Some countries have very few natural food resources. The inhabitants of these regions do not have enough knowledge to enable them to attain the same levels as the richer countries. They do not know how to cultivate the land; they are incapable of exploiting the potential which their country has to offer. And even when they know what to do, they often lack the means with which to do it. Industrialised countries give as much help to these countries as they possibly can: they send food, medicine and send out people to assess the situation. There also are many charitable organisations who send help to the developing countries. It is not enough, much more is needed. Sometimes, several agricultural machines or the construction of a water pipeline can be sufficient to start a village off.

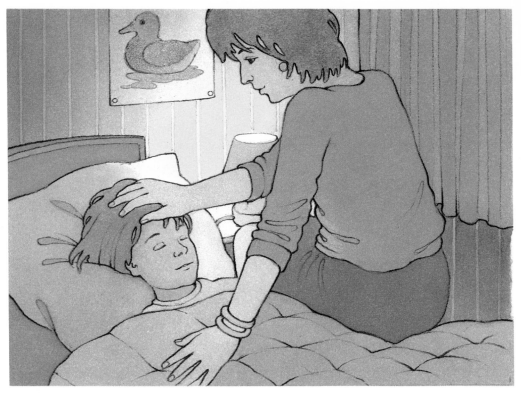

Sometimes your body does not function properly: it is ill.

Why are we sometimes ill?

The human body is very complex. Doctors already know a great deal, but the fact that each individual is different must always be taken into account. Illness is not only linked to the physical aspect of the body, but also to the feelings and mental processes taking place. To have an accident is not the same thing as being ill; in this instance, part of the body is injured or destroyed, but the state of being ill involves other elements too. You may catch 'flu or you may eat something which does not agree with you. Maybe one of your organs does not work so well for a period of time: you may have a pain in the back or be suffering from lack of sleep. Fortunately, you can be treated and cured, either at home or in hospital. However, it will take some time before everything works as well as it did before the illness. Nowadays, doctors are very well informed.

Why does the dark sometimes affect us?

Some people are not afraid of the dark. However, this depends to some extent on what is meant by dark. People move as a result of what they see with their eyes and not of what they hear, smell or touch, as animals do. But Man cannot see without light. We see nothing and feel uneasy in total darkness. What we call dark is not often completely so: most of the time there is a light around or the moon and stars provide some illumination. When you are in a familiar place, the light from the moon or a lamp is enough and you have no reason to be afraid. People often cause fear by telling frightening tales. However, you may feel uneasy when your surroundings are unfamiliar, because you don't know what obstacles you may meet. Many townspeople are frightened in woods and fields because they are used to the bright lights of the town. Countrypeople are often afraid when going into town.

Some people don't like to be out in the dark.

Why can't we fly like birds?

The body of a bird is completely different to that of a human being. It is designed to be carried by air. Birds have hollow backs supported inside by small partitions which are as hard as stone. Hence their frame is very light. Their feathered wings are strong and muscular and carry them up into the sky. Their body makes its way through the air offering very little resistance. A bird does not breathe in the same way as a human being does. A human body has a much heavier frame. It could not fly, even if wings were attached to it's back. Many have tried to do so, but all have failed. People who hang-glide or parachute are not flying in the true sense of the word. They cannot choose the direction in which they want to go or ascend or descend at will. As a result, Man used his intelligence to design planes capable of carrying him through the air.

A bird's body is designed so that it can fly.

Why do we have to work?

Each person responds to his needs. Some people, like fathers for example, take care of their families and see that they are provided for. So, they look for work to earn money to buy the things that they and their families need.

There are other reasons for working. A person may choose a particular job because he likes it and it makes him feel good. It is not always easy to find the job you like and in which you feel most comfortable, but it is worth looking for all the same.

Some jobs are better paid than others, but is it always best to look for a job which you like. Motivation is greater and there is less risk of turning into a money-making machine. Even if the job does not earn as much money, the person doing it will be much happier if he really enjoys it.

Everyone has needs to provide for: a job is the answer.

Why aren't animals endowed with reason?

First of all, let us define the expression "endowed with reason". The ability to do such things as use tools, tell a story, read a book or solve complex problems is all to do with reasoning. These are things which animals cannot do. However, some species, such as chimpanzees, are very gifted and learn quickly. Observers saw a chimpanzee work out all by himself how to slide one rod inside another to obtain a banana placed out of reach. Pigeons have been taught to push buttons and carry out small errands in exchange for food.

Despite many experiments and animal teaching programmes, none has ever passed the stage of evolution of a human baby. No animal can equal Man in this respect. Man has the ability to adapt to his environment and live in it, even though conditions of life may sometimes be very difficult.

Dolphins can perform complicated turns.

Birds communicate by whistling.

Why don't animals have the gift of speech?

Human language is the facility of making our thoughts known to others by means of sound. By means of language, you can arrange with a friend to go and build a camp next week. You can discuss what you will need for the project. You can also play with a group of friends, listen to a lesson or even hold a conference.

Animals cannot pursue any of these activities. However, they do have a kind of language of their own. Modern equipment has already detected a number of animal sounds imperceptible to the human ear.

Fish are not as quiet as we think either. They also emit sounds. Animal sounds are very varied and peculiar to each species. Scent and movement are also a type of language to them. Yet they are unable to speak like us because, amongst other things, they lack the speech organ, the vocal cords.

A dog perspires by panting.

Why does a dog's tongue hang out?

When you run or when you are in a hot country, your body gets rid of water: you perspire. Perspiration is of vital importance to the body: if you didn't sweat, you would get heatstroke. People who are unable to perspire after exertion or in a hot country have to find other means of cooling down.

When you perspire, small drops of water escape through pores in your skin. They evaporate quickly and your skin is dry again after a time. As the perspiration evaporates, it cools your body down and keeps your body temperature at 37°C (degrees Celsius).

Dogs cannot perspire through the skin, at least not to the same degree as humans do. But their tongue helps them to keep a constant body temperature. Evaporation is achieved by panting: rapid inhalation and exhalation.

Cats become attached to their home rather than their owner.

Why are cats disobedient?

Man already had domestic animals in the form of cattle a very long time ago. The oldest form of domestic animal in the areas in which we live is represented by livestock such as sheep and cows and smaller species such as rabbits. Dogs came later and became so domesticated subsequently that they were incapable of living without Man. At this time, our woods were populated by wild cats. Like all feline animals, they lived and hunted alone, apart from nesting with a mate. They defended their territory ferociously. The cat was one of the last animals to become domesticated in our country. Cats were living in homes during a much earlier period in Persia and Egypt. However, the cat does not need Man in order to survive; cats which have strayed and turned wild again look after themselves remarkably well. That is why they don't regard Man as their master and are not obedient.

Cow's milk is really meant for the calf.

Why does a cow give milk?

The cow belongs to the large family of mammals. All female mammals produce milk to succour their offspring as soon as the young one is born. Small mammals suck their mother's breasts, or udders in the case of a cow, in order to obtain food. The cow only produces milk after she has produced a calf. If the farmer wants a milking cow, he must see that she has a calf first. The first milk from a cow is different from ordinary milk and is called the colostrum. It is thicker and more sugary. The farmer lets the calf have the first milk, then he substitutes artificial milk, containing all the nutrients needed for the calf to thrive. Cow's milk contains all the substances necessary to human life. If a cow is to be a good milker, she must have a calf every year. There are different sorts of cows. A cow can give between 15 and 20 litres of milk per day, depending on breed.

Why do hens lay eggs?

Birds, including hens, lay eggs in order to produce chicks. Most birds still living in the wild have at least two sets of eggs each year, one in the spring and the other towards the end of the summer. It is different with hens. They lay an egg every day of the year, with a rest period of several months in between. This period is generally around Christmas, that is why eggs cost more at that time.

Each egg contains white and yolk. The yolk is the food element for the embryo which becomes a chick after it has hatched. The white acts as a protective layer. When the chick is big enough to leave, it breaks the shell of the egg which encloses it. It does this with a hard growth on its beak, which disappears as the chick grows up. This is called the "diamond". The hen sits on its egg for 21 days until the chick hatches out.

Battery hens lay up to 2 eggs per day.

Why does a camel have two humps?

Camels and their relatives, dromedaries, are called ungulates. They are capable of living in very dry regions. They are famous for their usefulness in the desert. They are known as "desert vehicles", as Man has used them for a very long time to transport goods across the deserts. The camel is equally at home in the oasis areas, where there is more vegetation and water.

The same thing happens with a camel as with us when we eat too much — layers of fat are formed. The camel builds up its reserves in its humps. The tissue making up the humps readily becomes liquid to supply the body with the essential humidity, when no drinking water is available. The camel's kidneys and intestines are also different from those of other mammals: not as much water is excreted. The camel urinates less. His excrement dries quickly and is used as a fire lighter.

A camel has two humps; a dromedary only has one.

Why do spiders make webs?

Spiders are ferocious animals. They feed off the flesh of insects and lower animals such as beetles and centipedes. Spiders belong to a large group. They are not insects, as the head and thorax form a whole. Thus, the body of a spider is made up of two parts: the cephalothorax and the abdomen. A spider has eight legs and no wings.

Spiders spin their webs from top to bottom or horizontally, close to the ground, like a sort of net. Some spiders spin very complex webs, incorporating traps, in the soil. The webs serve to trap prey and warn the spider when a catch has been made. The spider bites the prey in order to paralyze it and then keeps it in the web until all is peaceful and quiet. Finally, it sucks its prey out.

A spider often catches insects much bigger than itself as their wings catch in the mesh of the web.

A common garden spider weaves its pretty web.

Why has a tortoise got a shell?

One of the principle laws of nature is "eat or be eaten". The tortoise is vegetarian, so food is no great problem to him. Plants can't escape. But he must take care that he is not eaten by something else. Each animal defends itself in its own special way.

Tortoises belong to the same group of reptiles as crocodiles, snakes and lizards which have a thick skin and sometimes spines too. In the case of the tortoise, the skin on the back and stomach has hardened to become a kind of horned box with holes for the head, feet and small tail. The hooves of horses and cows are also made of horn. When danger threatens, the tortoise withdraws its head, feet and tail into its shell. The holes are then covered with a kind of skin plate as hard as the horn. The tortoise does not need to escape, he is well protected by his shell.

When danger threatens, the tortoise withdraws into its shell.

The baby elephant uses its trunk to hold on to its mother.

Why do elephants have trunks?

Various research programmes carried out have shown that elephants often use their trunks for different activities. Above all, they roll their trunks around leafy branches and remove them from the trees in this way. Then they slide the branches (which are often as thick as your arm) between their tusks and their trunk and break them before eating them. An elephant does not like to kneel down to drink water, therefore he uses his trunk. He sucks the water up into his trunk and then blows it out into his mouth. The trunk is also used as a shower head for washing. In this way, the body can be sprinkled with water. How wonderfully refreshing that must feel! The elephant sometimes sprinkles his body with mud: the mud dries and flakes or is rubbed off. In this way, the elephant can get rid of insects which bite him and thorns embedded in his skin.

Thanks to its long neck, the giraffe can always find food.

Why does a giraffe have such a long neck?

Plants are vital to every living thing on earth. Green plants manufacture nourishing products under the influence of the sun. Think of a potato which pushes up under the soil and is then dug up when the leaves dry off.

All vegetarian animals, and Man too, need greenery. Over the course of time, the different species have adapted to their natural environment. Differences between the various animals became apparent. Even now, changes are taking place in species and in their way of life.

An animal's food depends on the area in which it lives. A mole eats worms and mice; a hedgehog adores fallen fruit, decaying food and the like. Giraffes eat plants. They live in areas populated with vegetarians such as the antelope. Its long neck enables it to find food high up when there is a shortage at ground level.

The gills are just behind the eyes of the fish.

Why don't fish drown?

Like all other living creatures, plants as well as animals, fish need oxygen in order to survive. Their make-up allows them to take in oxygen from water. Water always contains dissolved oxygen in the same way as tea contains dissolved sugar; you can't see it, but it is easy to show it is there.

The colder the water, the more oxygen there is in it. When the water heats up, part of the oxygen escapes. Fish sometimes die in great numbers through lack of oxygen. Fish take in the oxygen they need through their gills. When you hold this book up by a corner and let the pages hang freely, then you get some idea of what gills look like. Gills are made up of a series of superimposed scales, which allow the water to filter through. Gills contain blood vessels which take oxygen from the water.

Stegosaurus was a prehistoric animal.

Why have prehistoric animals all disappeared?

Many theories have been put forward on this subject. No-one actually witnessed the extinction of prehistoric animals. No-one knows what really happened. However, at the present time, we are continuing to find signs which give some clues about the period. Animals such as the rhinoceros, hippopotamus and elephant are of special significance in view of their prehistoric character. Large animals require enormous quantities of food. This is becoming increasingly difficult to find, as Man is occupying more and more of the land for houses, roads and factories. Something similar could have happened before Man made his appearance on Earth. The territory occupied by the large reptiles could have become too small as a result of the various ice ages, during which part of the Earth was covered with ice. Or, maybe these animals were not able to adapt to the changing conditions.

Which is the fastest animal?

The cheetah is reputed to be the fastest animal in the world. This wild animal, which lives in the southern Sahara in Africa, hunts during the day. In contrast to other members of the cat family, the cheetah does not approach his prey stealthily, nor does he jump on it, but runs after and chases it. Its main source of food is antelope and deer. An antelope can also run very fast up to 100 km per hour, giving it a chance to escape from its predator.

Cheetahs run fast, but not for long periods. The cheetah may be the fastest animal in the world, but the black martin can fly at 280 km per hour; the petrel flies at 417 km per hour. The record for fish is held by the tuna, which can swim 100 km per hour. A horse gallops at about 40 km per hour. Some seasoned and well-trained runners do achieve these rates over short distances such as 100 metres.

Cheetahs can run in excess of 100 km per hour.

Which is the strongest animal?

The strongest animal on Earth is the elephant. There are two kinds of elephant: the African elephant (which has large ears) and the Indian elephant which has smaller ears and which is slightly smaller overall. A male African elephant may weigh up to 7000 kg. Man has often made use of an elephants strength. Indian elephants have been used as beasts of burden for centuries. They can uproot trees with their trunks and carry them to wherever is required.

Despite their enormous size, elephants are very gentle creatures and become very attached to their owners. Elephants are also used to transport people on tiger hunts. There are other large and powerful land mammals such as the rhinoceros. The rhinoceros is the second heaviest and most powerful animal. Whales are also very powerful creatures.

The elephant is the strongest animal in the world.

Why do plants need water and fertilizers?

Plants need water and food in the same way as all other living things do. They are readily available in nature. The various kinds of plants grow in the types of soil containing the nutrients which they need. After a certain time, the food supply becomes exhausted and the plant is superceded by a different type with different food requirements. In the wild, the various types of plant succeed each other naturally, without the need for chemical fertilizer, without manure. A plant derives as much nourishment from the surface of the soil as it does from the ground underneath. The leaves take in carbon dioxide from the air and give out oxygen. The root system takes in the nourishing salts contained in the water which has drained through. Sometimes, the soil will become impoverished in gardens where there is no crop rotation and the owner puts in what he pleases. In this case, fertilizers are needed.

Plants also have their needs.

How can poisonous mushrooms be recognised?

Unfortunately, there is no rule for recognising poisonous mushrooms. If you want to eat mushrooms, it is best to buy them or to cultivate them in wooden troughs, which is a very popular activity at the present time. You should not eat wild mushrooms unless someone who knows about them has taught you how to recognize them, or has checked them after picking. However, edible mushroom picking has made certain species rare and in danger of disappearing altogether. This provides a very good reason for not picking mushrooms at all. Neither should you pick them to make a collection. If you want to see mushrooms, look at them in the wild, but do not touch them, pick them, knock them over or crush them.

Most yellow mushrooms belong to the amanite family, as do the red ones with white spots. They are all poisonous and can be deadly.

The amanite is one of the most dangerous mushrooms.

The foliage of a tree takes up a lot of space.

Why do trees have leaves?

Trees need food which they take in through their roots and their leaves. But the leaves have other roles to play. The underground roots of a tree are spread out so that the distance between the trunk and the fine underground network is equal to the height of the tree. When it rains, droplets fall on the top of the tree, slip from branch to branch (without wetting the trunk) and fall on to the ground, penetrating the soil from which the moisture is absorbed by the root ends. When the sun shines, the trunk is protected by the foliage. If there were no foliage, the trunk would break like a matchstick during very hot periods. The effect of very strong and persistant sun on a non-shaded trunk is the same as that of an axe: the bark and the branches fall and finally the trunk breaks up. The leaves form a type of large roof to prevent this. They also play a part in the respiration process of the tree.

55

Rowan berries have a beautiful reddish-coral colour.

Why do some plants have berries?

Most plants with berries are shrubs. In the wild, most bushes - such as the elder and the rowan - grow in between the large trees. A wood is made up of 4 constituent parts: the layer of humus, incorporating leaves and rotting vegetation; a grass layer which is on the ground and may or may not contain flowers; the bushes which are scattered about, and finally the trees which form the highest layer of all. When there are too many trees, the grass and bushes are stifled. But this rarely happens.

Wild blackberries and raspberries can grow through the densest wood. The birds eat the berries and scatter the undigested part of the plant, the seeds, several miles away as part of their excrement. These seeds come to rest in open spaces where they germinate and grow into new bushes.

Wild flowers are often very pretty.

Why should wild flowers not be picked?

The law protects many kinds of wild flowers. If you disobey the law, you will have to pay a fine. The law seeks to prevent the disappearance of rare species. It is better not to pick even those flowers which are not protected, as they do not last very long and have to be thrown out any-way. If no-one picks wild flowers, everyone can enjoy them and the species will not be endangered.

When you pick a flower, there will be no fruit, no berries, no seeds, no new plant the following spring and the species will probably die out in the more, or less, distant future.

This applies to annual or biennial plants in particular. This means that one or two years must pass before the seed grows into a plant which will flower and bear fruit. If the plant is picked, there will be no seed and the plant will not grow again the following year.

Pretty coloured perfumed roses are protected by thorns.

Why do some plants have thorns?

When a fruit nurseryman wants to protect the beautiful pears and apples in his orchard from vandals, he surrounds the area with barbed wire. When a farmer or nurseryman wants to keep cows, sheep and deer away from the plants or the young trees in his field, he also puts up a barbed wire fence. The sharp points keep animals away. This is of special importance in regions which have very few plants and a lot of animals, such as deserts, savanna and steppe lands. Nature has provided the vegetation in these areas with sharp thorns. The cactus provides a very good example of this. Plants in our country which grow in sandy areas obey the same law: the buckthorn, the blackthorn and the hawthorn all have long sharp thorns. The rose, which is the flower of an ornamental shrub, is also protected by thorns. These are possibly provided to make sure that prying fingers keep their distance.

How is paper made?

Most of the time, paper is a 100 % natural product. It is made from wood. Papyrus rolls from papyrus leaves used to be used in the Middle East at the beginning of this era. Well before that, the Chinese used to write on rice paper. Europeans used parchment: treated animal skins.

Nowadays, cheap paper is made from wood or from textile fibres such as wool, linen or cotton. Old paper can be recycled. The wood or textile fibres are crushed, washed and baked; they are then mixed with water to make a paste. Kneaded, dissolved, baked and mixed with water, the paste is then refined. Certain products are added to make the paper smoother and more supple. The paste is then poured into a kind of strainer, pressed and dried until a sheet of paper emerges, on which you can write again.

The paste is dried and pressed to give sheets of paper.

How does a telephone work?

You lift up the receiver and dial a number. A complex system of wires and cables sends electric impulses corresponding to the number you have just dialled on your dial to a telephone exchange. The exchange forwards these impulses to the telephone corresponding to the required number by means of further wires and cables. At this moment, the electric current sent down the line activates the bell. The person called only has to pick up his receiver for contact to be made. When calling another area, the impulses may pass through two exchanges. These are called relays. The sensitive capsules in the receiver, one in the earpiece, the other in the mouthpiece, enable you to talk to someone at the end of another telephone. When you speak, the "mouth" capsule in your receiver vibrates and sends electric impulses to the "ear" capsule at the other end. The person listening then hears you talk.

We can communicate easily by telephone.

How does a car go?

Cylinders are responsible for the running of a car: these are hollow spaces in which a fuel (petrol, fuel oil or gas) is fired by a spark which causes it to explode. As the cylinders are small, the explosion gives rise to considerable pressure. One of the cylinder walls is mobile: the piston. The force of the explosion pushes the piston upwards. The petrol which explodes successively causes each piston to move. The successive piston movements are transmitted to a special shaft (the drive-shaft). The shaft begins to turn. As the shaft rotates, the movement is transmitted to the front and back wheels by a series of shafts and cogs. The transmission unit also incorporates the gear box, the clutch and the rear axle. The gear box allows the driver to control the energy transmitted from the engine to the wheels. If you accelerate quickly, the fuel explodes faster so the car travels faster.

Man is always trying to go faster.

Where does the water in the pipes come from?

This depends on the area in which you live. If you live near a big lake, a river or a pond, your water probably comes from there. However, with all the water pollution nowadays, it will be treated in a water purification plant before being used. Polders are other areas which are well supplied with water. Polders are generally found in natural regions and woodland areas. Underground water is pumped up and treated. This is simply rain water absorbed by the ground. This water is purer because it has already been filtered by various layers of soil.
At the present time, river water is passed over filter beds, such as dunes. The sand is an excellent water filter, and the water passing through then goes to the pumping station to be further purified into drinking water. This water is then pumped to reservoirs built on raised ground, and from there it is relayed to the pipes in your home.

A purification plant makes water fit to drink.

Food keeps longer in the refrigerator.

Why do we keep food in the refrigerator?

Our food is the home for quite a lot of small living germs which feed off it too. In general, we do not know they exist; they can only be seen under a microscope and are inoffensive. If the food that we eat is fresh, the germs, mildew and bacteria, do not present any danger. They are eliminated in excrement or killed in either the stomach or the intestines. When the food has been kept for several days, it becomes stale and germs develop. They develop much more readily if the food is kept in an ambient temperature than if it is put into a humid atmosphere. Take a look at butter or ageing fruit: you will see mildew appear. We say that the food is rotten. One or two days is enough. If the food is kept in the refrigerator, the germs can not change into mildew and bacteria so quickly and remain inoffensive for longer, as they are not at the temperature in which they thrive best.

The engines and wings keep the aeroplane in the air.

How do aeroplanes fly?

The make-up of a bird allows it to soar in the sky. Some species such as eagles and buzzards have such large wings that they scarcely have to flap them at all to stay up. The shape of our aeroplanes was inspired by that of birds. The front of normal aeroplanes is fitted with one or two propellers. When they turn, they move away the air to create a vacuum. As the air exerts a pressure over the whole fuselage, the aeroplane is kept up in the sky by the pressure difference between front and back. As long as the propellers turn, the aeroplane stays in the sky and moves forward. In jet aeroplanes, the engines draw the air in and push it out towards the back. The aeroplane can fly faster and keep its balance in the air better. The wings and the tail of the machine are fitted with flaps, by means of which the craft is steered. Progress in the field of aviation is proceeding at an astronomical rate.

The large cooling towers are indispensable.

Is nuclear energy really dangerous?

Yes, but we would hasten to add that all other forms of energy are also dangerous. Atomic or nuclear energy is chiefly used in the production of electricity. Electricity can also be obtained by boiling oil, petroleum or natural gas to heat water up to evaporation point. The steam turns the turbines, machines which produce the electricity. The gas and soot resulting from combustion are toxic to Man, animals and plants. When all is running smoothly, a nuclear plant emits only an excess of heat which is easy to control. However, no satisfactory solution has yet been found for the radio-active waste which is also produced. The greatest risk lies in a breakdown of the plant: radio-active products which could damage our health and even threaten our lives could be released. However, you can rest assured that safety and intervention to be carried out in the event of a breakdown, have been worked out.

Cables carry electricity produced at the power stations.

What is electricity?

We shall start by taking a look at water: turn on a tap. A jet of water gushes out under the pressure exerted by pumps on the water in the pipes. Once the water has left the tap, the pressure drops sharply, hence the water emerges in the form of a jet. Now let us consider a battery. On the one side, you can see the sign +, that means that the particles of electricity are pumped. There is an electric pressure. The sign - is seen on the other side, and here there is no electric force. The electrons, the name given to electric particles, move from + to -, just as water runs from the tap into the sink. Electricity is produced at a power station by magnets which turn around each other. As the magnetic forces change, the electrons move along the copper wire, thus producing electricity. Electricity is taken to your homes by the cables which you can see along the roadsides.

What are aerials for?

Another word for aerial is antenna. This is a word also used in bio-logy. Insects have antennae with which they can touch, feel and hear. The antennae or aerials fixed on rooftops do the same thing. They listen to the sky and sometimes up in space too, to try and capture radio waves. Radio waves are magnetic vibrations which cross the sky, not the air. Air is not essential for radio waves. There are different sorts of waves, the form of which is determined by the emitter. All sorts of waves can be sent by the transmitter mast. Electrical waves and signals can be transformed if you have a receiver. This in its turn transmits electric impulses to a loud speaker or to a screen. There are different emitters and receivers for radio, television etc, in the same way as there are different sorts of waves. These emitters and receivers are known as aerials.

Aerials are used for emitting and receiving radio waves.

INDEX